IT'S TIME TO EAT RAISINS

It's Time to Eat RAISINS

Walter the Educator

Silent King Books
A WhichHead Entertainment Imprint

Copyright © 2024 by Walter the Educator

All rights reserved. No part of this book may be reproduced in any manner whatsoever without written per- mission except in the case of brief quotations embodied in critical articles and reviews.

First Printing, 2024

Disclaimer

This book is a literary work; the story is not about specific persons, locations, situations, and/or circumstances unless mentioned in a historical context. Any resemblance to real persons, locations, situations, and/or circumstances is coincidental. This book is for entertainment and informational purposes only. The author and publisher offer this information without warranties expressed or implied. No matter the grounds, neither the author nor the publisher will be accountable for any losses, injuries, or other damages caused by the reader's use of this book. The use of this book acknowledges an understanding and acceptance of this disclaimer.

It's Time to Eat RAISINS is a collectible early learning book by Walter the Educator suitable for all ages belonging to Walter the Educator's Time to Eat Book Series. Collect more books at WaltertheEducator.com

USE THE EXTRA SPACE TO TAKE NOTES AND DOCUMENT YOUR MEMORIES

RAISINS

It's time to eat, come gather near,

It's Time to Eat
Raisins

A tiny treat we all hold dear.

Wrinkly, sweet, and full of fun,

Raisins are great for everyone!

They started as grapes upon the vine,

Soaking in sunshine, feeling fine.

Then they dried in the golden sun,

Becoming raisins for everyone!

In a box or bowl, they love to stay,

Ready to snack on any day.

Pop them in and taste the cheer,

A tiny burst of flavor's here!

Take them along wherever you go,

A snack for hikes or playtime's flow.

In your pocket, they're a friend,

Raisins bring joy that doesn't end.

It's Time to Eat
Raisins

Add them to oatmeal, warm and sweet,

Or sprinkle on cookies for a treat.

In muffins or bread, they love to hide,

Raisins make every bite a surprise!

They're healthy too, so good for you,

With vitamins and fiber too.

Energy packed in every bite,

Raisins keep you feeling bright.

Purple, golden, small, and neat,

Raisins are the perfect treat.

No mess, no fuss, just open wide,

Snack time is fun with raisins inside!

They're little, but don't be fooled, you see,

They're packed with power and energy.

For running, jumping, climbing, and play,

It's Time to Eat
Raisins

Raisins give strength throughout the day!

Let's all shout, "Hooray, hooray!"

For raisins brightening up our day.

From breakfast time to evening's end,

Raisins are our tasty friend.

So grab a handful, don't delay,

It's raisin time, hooray, hooray!

A snack so sweet, so pure, so small,

It's Time to Eat
Raisins

Raisins are the best of all!

ABOUT THE CREATOR

Walter the Educator is one of the pseudonyms for Walter Anderson. Formally educated in Chemistry, Business, and Education, he is an educator, an author, a diverse entrepreneur, and he is the son of a disabled war veteran. "Walter the Educator" shares his time between educating and creating. He holds interests and owns several creative projects that entertain, enlighten, enhance, and educate, hoping to inspire and motivate you. Follow, find new works, and stay up to date with Walter the Educator™

at WaltertheEducator.com

www.ingramcontent.com/pod-product-compliance
Lightning Source LLC
LaVergne TN
LVHW052014060526
838201LV00059B/4029